Energizers

FOR TRAINING AND CONFERENCES

John E. Jones, Ph.D.
William L. Bearley, Ed.D.

ENERGIZERS

FOR TRAINING AND CONFERENCES

**Organization Design
and Development, Inc.**
King of Prussia, Pennsylvania

Contents

Preface

We are inveterate collectors of training tools. And we like sharing them with others. Hence this little book on energizers. We searched our files and consciousnesses, finding a rich array of ways to elevate group energy. Our aims here are to make those techniques available to many and to stimulate further such sharing among professionals in human resource development.

Jack Carew, Joe Cascarelli, and Andy Sloan of Carew Positional Selling Systems introduced us to several of the activities in this collection, and we are grateful for their cooperation. Also, we are indebted to our consulting clients who, over many years, have permitted us to experiment with their people as we have developed contributions to the emerging technology of our field. We give special thanks to Eric Barbour, Joe Cascarelli, Colleen Kelley, Carol Roberts, and Peter Rutherford for their suggestions on improving the manuscript.

The original sources of most of the ideas contained in these energizers are unknown. They are part of the "folk music" of training. Some people may claim credit for them, but it is our experience that after trainers and presenters have used a method for a while, they think they invented it! If you think you did create one of these techniques, please accept our apology in advance for not having credited you properly.

We are interested in enlarging our repertoire of energizers. If you have some that are not included here, send them so that we can include them in future editions.

San Diego, California
December, 1989

Using Energizers in Training Sessions and Conferences

This book contains numerous activities that trainers and other presenters can use in a wide variety of settings. Before we get into the theory and technology of using energizers, let us make some distinctions among terms that are often confused.

There are "three bags full" of activities commonly used to enliven training: ice-breakers, getting acquainted exercises, and energizers. We believe that, although there is undoubtedly some overlap in these categories, these three types of activities are distinctly different.

Ice-breakers take place first thing in training events and conferences. They are whatever you do to establish contact with the group or audience and to get participants to join the experience with you. The Pfeiffer & Jones *Handbooks* and *Annuals* (1972-1981) contain dozens of ice-breaking activities.

Getting acquainted exercises do just what their category name implies. They get participants acquainted with one another. Hart's *Saying Hello* (1989) includes many designs for this purpose.

Energizers are activities that raise the energy level of participants. They may be used at any time during a training event or conference. This book focuses solely on these techniques.

Purposes of Using Energizers

The overall purpose of using energizers is, of course, to raise the energy level of the group. Other purposes are:

To promote readiness for learning. Participants do not learn well when they have low energy. Sluggishness can lead to inattentiveness, and the phenomenon can be contagious within a group. Slouching in chairs, leaning on tables, and other nonverbal behaviors can be subliminally observed and copied by other group members. Energizers can get participants ready to engage your material.

To create excitement. You should be excited about the content of your training event or conference. That does not mean that your participants are equally stimulated. Learning is exciting to children, but adults sometimes seem not to want the experience. Energizers can generate a positive expectation of upcoming training and conference events.

To overcome the effects of fatigue, drowsiness, and drag. Long days, hot rooms, difficult material — all these can put participants in a kind of mild stupor. Energizers can "wake them up" to go on with the program refreshed.

To develop a sense of shared fun. You can facilitate even the most serious deliberations with comic relief, as long as you keep a proper perspective on the proceedings. An occasional group laugh can make any session more lively.

Characteristics of Energizers

Your imagination sets the limit on what is possible to use as an energizer. The activities in this book have several characteristics in common. Most of them are "content-free," that is, participants do not learn anything while participating in them. However, we include several that make a point, in the context of fun.

Energizers often involve physical movement of some sort. Trainers in Japan use videotaped calisthenics. When the session becomes tiresome, the Trainer calls for exercise, the participants rise as a group, and everyone follows the videotaped instructions for a few minutes. We favor less rigid designs, and the energizers we chose for this book tend to emphasize interaction as well as movement. The simplest energizer is to have participants stand and stretch, or stretch (even push and shove) one another.

Energizers are, or should be, quick. Some of them can take so much time as to actually increase fatigue. The activities we use most often take one to five minutes.

Energizers are often competitive. Many participants seem programmed to win in win-lose exercises. Competitive energizers capitalize on this trait by using it to raise energy.

Adults can profit from "regressive" activities that permit and encourage them to act as children for a brief moment. Energizers that involve play are especially useful in any problem solving and action-planning sessions in which creativity is desirable.

Energizers often involve having participants use their imaginations. This can lead to more open thinking, receptivity to new ideas and information, and heightened creativity.

Creating Your Own Energizers

You can make up energizers easily. Get ideas from children's games, current events, television shows, or other sources. Follow the points discussed above, and use your imagination. Start with a clear purpose (usually to raise energy). Then select objects, movements, interactions, and staging that will achieve your objective. Keep the activity quick and energetic.

We provide ideas for variations for all of the energizers in this collection. You may think of others. Space is provided for you to record your ideas, along with your use of the ones presented here.

When to Use Energizers

These activities are not just "throw-ins," randomly inserted into the proceedings. They are purposeful, and they need to be used strategically. There are *three* times when using energizers can greatly enhance the impact of training and conferences: just after a meal, after a refreshment break, and when a long session begins to drag. These are the most common times when participants are likely to be "de-energized," or less than optimally ready to go on with the program. You may actually reduce the impact of your session by overusing these activities or by using them at the wrong times.

Style in Using Energizers

In using these activities it is important to model the results you are after. You must be energetic yourself for them to work well. Your style should be upbeat and positive. Put a little mystery into your introduction of the energizer. We say something like, "I feel confident that you will find that what we are about to do will be interesting, stimulating, useful, involving, portable, and memorable!" Because we say that often in training events and conferences, participants begin to pick it up and say it back to us in fun, of course.

The Trainer should participate in energizers whenever appropriate. This can bond you to the group, and it can keep you physically and mentally ready to do an effective job as a presenter. By all means, whether you participate or not, have fun with them!

Cautions

Remember that the purpose of training events and conferences usually is not simply to have a good time. Keep the learning and productivity goals in mind as you make adjustments to your program design. Include energizers judiciously.

Some energizers that feature physical movement involve safety considerations. You need to take reasonable precautions in using these activities. You may need to rearrange the furniture, invite participants to choose whether they will do the activity, and make certain that it is not unduly strenuous.

Keep these activities short. Their length varies, but do not let them go on for too long. Some participants will want you to do nothing but "content-free" exercises, but resist the temptation. Unless you are primarily an entertainer, keep your energizers brief and move back to your material quickly.

Using energizers in training events and conferences can generate a norm of play instead of productive work. They can enliven a dull session, but they can also result in an expectation of superficiality in the proceedings. People can spontaneously "laugh off" serious topics, while keeping up a group norm of always having a good time.

Another potential negative outcome of using energizers is that they can contribute to a norm of competitiveness. This atmosphere can make collaboration and interpersonal support difficult.

Some participants see energizers as "Ding-Dong School." Many activities are, in fact, a bit silly. The way we defuse participants is to tell them in advance, "What we are about to do may *look* silly, but we will all be doing it, so what's the difference?"

Using energizers inappropriately can divert attention away from issues. Keep their purpose in mind, and repeatedly emphasize the overarching goals of the session.

Being cautious in using energizers must not interfere with your style in actually running them. A lot of their success comes from the Trainer's frame of mind and skill in setting them up effectively. You do yourself, and your participants, a great service in keeping the session interesting and stimulating.

ALL MY FRIENDS

Summary This is a highly active exercise that gets participants up and moving in a fun way. They sit on chairs in a circle and move rapidly to different chairs as the person who is "it" gives them a cue.

Preparation None

Procedure

1. Have participants sit in a broad circle, with exactly enough chairs for everyone except you. Stand in the center of the circle.

2. Spell out the procedure for the game. Only the people who fit the characteristic named by the person in the center must get up and move to a vacated chair. The person who is "it" should also try to occupy a vacated chair. The one left standing will then be "it" and will give the next characteristic, and so on. The "characteristic" is announced in a sentence that begins, "All my friends..."

3. Use these two examples as practice rounds, and remain standing yourself so that you are "it" in the second round. Round 1: "All my friends like money!" Round 2: "All my friends like chocolate!" (Do your best to get a chair during Round 2.)

4. The person who is left standing after the practice rounds then makes a statement beginning with, "All my friends..." For example, "All my friends are left-handed." "All my friends ate sausage this morning."

5. Let the rounds continue for three or four minutes.

Cautions We have paid for a few chairs as a result of doing this energizer. It helps if you begin with sturdy, inexpensive furniture. People become animated during the chair changes.

Warn people who may have physical constraints not to participate but to observe and get in on the fun.

Variations
- The statement can be different. For example, "I like people who..." It may even be a question such as, "Who has had a promotion in the last year?"

- You can establish the rule that the person who is "it" must be in the center of the circle when making the statement. (An easy way to get out of the center is to stand close to someone who has the characteristic that you are about to name.)

Usage

Group: Date:
Comments:

Group: Date:
Comments:

Group: Date:
Comments:

Group: Date:
Comments:

Group: Date:
Comments:

Ideas for Variations

BALLS OF YARN

Summary This activity gets participants all tangled up in soft yarn and then requires them to extricate themselves.

Preparation Obtain two or more balls of yarn in different colors.

Procedure
1. Announce that this activity will be a lot of fun. Get participants to stand in a large circle, facing one another. Give the balls of yarn to people who are far apart and ask them to hold the yarn until you say, "Go!"

2. Explain that the group will be making a spider web with the yarn. The people with the yarn balls hold the end of the string and gently throw the balls across the group to someone else. Then those people hold the string and throw the balls to a third person, and so on, until the balls have been completely unwound.

3. Ask for questions, answer them, and then say, "Go!"

4. When the yarn is unrolled completely, announce that they will now reverse the process until the balls are completely rewound. (Do not announce in the beginning that you will be asking them to do this.)

5. Have the group congratulate itself on accomplishing the task.

Cautions None

Variations
*   Have the group sing while it is doing the task. (This is a great holiday office party activity, with sing-along music playing in the background.)

*   Instead of throwing the yarn balls across the circle, the group can tie itself up into a large knot with the yarn and then undo itself.

Usage   Group: Date:
            Comments:

            Group: Date:
            Comments:

            Group: Date:
            Comments:

            Group: Date:
            Comments:

            Group: Date:
            Comments:

Ideas for Variations

BARNYARD

Summary   Groups find each other by making the sounds of assigned animals.

Preparation   None

Procedure   1. Announce that the next activity will get everyone up and moving in a unique way. Have everyone stand and close their eyes.

2. Point out that you will be moving among the group, touching each person on the shoulder and assigning an animal to him or her. Tell them to keep their eyes closed until the game is over.

3. Go to the participants, one at a time, touch them on the shoulder, and tell them the animal type that they will be. (You can use any animal that has a distinctive sound, such as a pig, chicken, rooster, cow, horse, dog, sheep, or donkey. You want groups of about eight to ten for each animal, so select the number of animals by dividing the group by eight, nine, or ten.)

4. Tell them that their task is to find one another while keeping their eyes closed and making the sound of their assigned animal.

Cautions   Get all of the furniture out of the way for this energizer so that people do not bump into it.

If two or more groups with the same animal designation form, you may have to steer one group in the direction of the other.

Variations   You may give each person a card with a number on it as they enter the room. Later you can explain that the 1's will be cows, the 2's will be chickens, etc. You may arrange the animal groups in the corners of the room, while you stand in the center. Each group makes the sound of its assigned animal as loudly as possible. You judge the winner. (This is usually a dead heat.) Ask people afterward how they felt (usually foolish). This energizer can introduce discussions about risk taking, creativity, self-expression, or change.

Usage   Group: Date:

Comments:

Group: Date:

Comments:

Group: Date:

Comments:

Group: Date:

Comments:

Group: Date:

Comments:

Ideas for Variations

BASKETBALL CARRY

Summary   This activity gets participants to cooperate in teams to carry basketballs across the floor on circular platforms.

Preparation   Obtain one basketball (or soccer or playground ball) for each team of six to eight people.

Construct a circular "carrying platform" – approximately four feet in diameter – for each team. It can be made from plywood or heavy cardboard. Attach four four-foot ropes around the platform, evenly spaced. You can vary the number of four-foot ropes on the platform.

Procedure   1. In a large room, place the platforms on the floor in separate locations for each team (as far apart as possible). Assemble one team around each platform.

2. Give each team a ball, and tell them to place the ball on the platform and raise it three feet by using the ropes.

3. If there are more than six participants in each team, repeat the exercise, having them pass the ropes to other group members while the platform is raised.

4. Next, have pairs of teams elevate their platforms (with the balls), cross the room toward each other, and return.

5. Finally, have all teams *simultaneously* cross the room and return, as before, but *without talking*.

Cautions   None

Variations   • Reduce the size of the platforms and have two- or three-person teams, perhaps using smaller balls.

• Call time-out before the final round and get the group to organize itself for the task.

Usage   Group: Date:
              Comments:

              Group: Date:
              Comments:

              Group: Date:
              Comments:

              Group: Date:
              Comments:

              Group: Date:
              Comments:

Ideas for Variations

BIG APPLE

Summary   Participants make the sounds of New York City on a Saturday night.

Preparation   None

Procedure
1. Explain that this exercise will require the participants to use their imaginations and expressive abilities. They are to create the sounds of New York City on a Saturday night. Explain that if someone has never been there, they can imagine it or remember it from the movies and television.

2. Call for a volunteer to make one of the sounds and to keep making that sound throughout the exercise. Then call for another volunteer to make a different sound. Then another and another, until everyone is involved.

3. Finally, tell participants to slowly diminish as the night fades into memory, dropping out one by one.

4. Ask for a round of applause for everyone.

Cautions   None

Variations   Have teams coach their individual members on different sounds before starting the scene. If they have a sequence of sounds to make, have them number off in order to make their entries organized.

Usage   Group: Date:
              Comments:

              Group: Date:
              Comments:

              Group: Date:
              Comments:

Group: Date:
Comments:

Group: Date:
Comments:

Ideas for Variations

BINGO

Summary   Participants mill around to find "matches" until they fill in five names in a row on their Bingo card.

Preparation   Make up an activity card or worksheet, such as the following, with one copy for each participant. Make sure that everyone has a pencil or pen.

Democrat	Left-handed	Divorced	Younger	New Age
New	Leo	Bird watcher	Introvert	Republican
Skeptic	Cheerleader	FREE	Cook	Golfer
Collector	Natural Leader	Good with math	Host	Cat lover
Gardener	Hockey fan	Shopper	Saver	Fixer-upper

Procedure   1. Tell everyone that before going on with the program, they are going to learn something important about each other.

2. Distribute the Bingo cards and explain that to win the game they must find people who fit the descriptions on the card and write their names in the squares. Only one "match" per participant is permitted. When they get five in a row, including the FREE space, they are to stop and yell "Bingo!"

3. Start the process. When almost all participants have finished, ask the remaining ones to seek their "matches" out loud. Get applause for each matching and especially for each Bingo.

Cautions   None

Variations

- You can choose almost any tasteful category to put into the squares of the card. This might include company-specific items, information that you know about each person, etc.

- The activity can be taken out of the Bingo mode, and you can instruct people to fill their entire cards in a specified amount of time.

- Find out interesting facts about each person during the early stage of your training event or conference. Use these facts to make up Bingo cards. With very large groups you may want to create more than one card.

Usage   Group: Date:
Comments:

Group: Date:
Comments:

Group: Date:
Comments:

Group: Date:
Comments:

Group: Date:
Comments:

Ideas for Variations

We built this energizer on an idea given to us by Fran Sims, Suncoast Management Institute, St. Petersburg, Florida.

BUMPERQUACK

Summary   This silly activity requires participants to act like imaginary animals while seeking to escape from a big circle.

Preparation   None

Procedure

1. "Bumperquack" can be carried out in a large space inside as well as outdoors. Get the group into a large circle and have participants count off by twos. Instruct the "1's" to form an inner circle. Have an outer circle of "2's" close in around them.

2. Describe the mythical "bumperquack." This is an animal with strange behavior. It only moves backwards while holding its heels, keeping its eyes closed, and yelling "Quack!" You may wish to illustrate the behavior.

3. Explain that members of the inner circle will be bumperquacks and that their goal is to escape the circle by finding the "hole in the fence." Once they are out, they are free to join the outer circle as "humanoid life forms."

4. Tell members of the outer circle that they may assist the bumperquacks by gently bumping them toward the opening. Explain that you will create the opening after the bumperquacks have closed their eyes.

5. Ask the bumperquacks to begin acting like themselves. Then quickly create a hole in the outer circle and help the outside members bump the bumperquacks toward it.

6. As people get outside the circle, direct them to help bump the remaining bumperquacks until all are out.

7. Repeat the process by reversing the inner and outer circle members.

Cautions   This activity can be strenuous for some people, particularly ones with little physical flexibility. Let these people simply bend over a little and put their hands on their thighs, if they need to. Ask anyone with a bad back not to participate in the inner circle.

Keep the energizer moving quickly, because it can consume quite a bit of time if you let it. For very large groups, run the activity simultaneously in two places.

Variations   • Other behavior can be substituted for what is prescribed for the bumperquacks. For example, they could be "Bumpersnorts" or "Bottomwhooshes."

• Have more than one hole in the fence. Wait two or three minutes before making another opening.

Usage   Group: Date:
Comments:

Group: Date:
Comments:

Group: Date:
Comments:

Group: Date:
Comments:

Group: Date:
Comments:

Ideas for Variations

CHARADES

Summary   Teams compete with one another to guess what the others portray.

Preparation   Generate a list of unusual events/happenings/processes for teams to act out. Here are some examples:

> Corn growing
> Putting together a bicycle on Christmas Eve
> Cooking an artichoke.

Procedure   1. Announce that teams will compete in a fun activity that is a variation of charades. Assemble the teams apart from each other in the room, and assign a topic for each to portray without words.

2. Allow two minutes for teams to create ways of portraying their assigned topics.

3. Call for a volunteer team to act out its topic, and then ask the remaining teams to ask questions in the familiar "charades" manner.

4. Teams guess what topic is being portrayed. Finally, have the team give the correct answer in its own way.

5. Give points to teams whose topics are guessed correctly, along with similar points to the team(s) that guesses correctly. Give more points for quick, correct answers.

6. Repeat the process until all teams have portrayed their topics.

Cautions   Keep the topics tasteful and fun.

Variations   • Have the teams make up their own topics.

• Allow no questions. (This method is much quicker.)

• Instead of the charades format you can use the rules and procedure of the commercially available Pictionary game or the television show "Win, Lose, or Draw."

Usage   Group: Date:
             Comments:

             Group: Date:
             Comments:

             Group: Date:
             Comments:

             Group: Date:
             Comments:

             Group: Date:
             Comments:

Ideas for Variations

COMPUTERS

Summary   Teams act as computers while answering questions in a special way.

Preparation   None

Procedure

1. Assemble teams of six to eight members with each team sitting in a circle.

2. Explain that each group is now a computer, and it can only respond to queries as a computer would, one word at a time. Choose a team to illustrate. Stand behind one member, who will give the first word of the answer. Others build up the answer clockwise, one word per member, until a "complete" answer is produced. Start with a sample question such as, "What is the meaning of life?" Have the chosen team respond.

3. Now explain that there will be a practice round for all computers. Have each group select a starter. The answer will proceed clockwise, beginning with the starter. Ask a practice question, such as, "How high is up?" Have all teams answer simultaneously.

4. Explain that these computers also complete unfinished sentences. Give an example: "As managers, women..." Ask for a volunteer computer to complete the sentence. Call for a round of applause. Then have all groups simultaneously complete this sentence (or another of your choosing): "The difference between managers and leaders is..."

5. Announce that the final round will be answers to questions or sentence completions across groups. Instruct them to talk like humans for a minute to come up with either a question or an interesting incomplete sentence.

6. Announce that teams are computers again and that they will give or respond to the questions or incomplete sentences one word at a time, one person per word, beginning with the starter and proceeding clockwise. Assign one team to answer another's query (or complete its incomplete sentence) going around the room in sequence. (Team 2 responds to Team 1, Team 3 to Team 2, and so on.)

7. Ask for a round of applause for each of the answers.

Cautions
This activity could drag. Keep it moving briskly. If a team gets stuck, move on and come back to them.

Make sure that the questions and incomplete sentences are tasteful and fun. Do not let the activity become serious.

Variations
- You can save time by omitting the incomplete sentences feature.

- You may use fun items from your organization, even employing actual names of prominent people.

Usage

Group: Date:
Comments:

Group: Date:
Comments:

Group: Date:
Comments:

Group: Date:
Comments:

Group: Date:
Comments:

Ideas for Variations

COUNTING F'S

Summary   This quick energizer simply requires participants to count the number of F's in a sentence.

Preparation   Get ready to show the sentence. You could write it on an overhead transparency or on a flipchart or whiteboard. Keep it hidden until the last second. Write the sentence all in capital letters:

> FINISHED FILES ARE THE RESULT OF YEARS OF SCIENTIFIC
> STUDY COMBINED WITH THE EXPERIENCE OF MANY YEARS.

Procedure   1. Tell participants to get paper and pencils or pens ready to do a simple and interesting task.

2. When everyone is ready, tell them that they are to do the task quickly, without talking. Then instruct them to count the number of F's in the sentence you are about to show. Ask them to write down the number on a scrap of paper.

3. Reveal the sentence and wait for about thirty seconds. Remove the sentence and ask everyone to write down the number of F's.

4. Ask for a volunteer answer and get a show of hands of all those who wrote the same number. Get another answer and another show of hands. Continue until you have all answers.

5. Then reshow the sentence. Ask how people could have different answers. (The gimmick is that people tend not to count the F in "of," because it is pronounced as a V.)

Cautions   None

Variations   Rewrite the sentence to suit your purposes. You may even include organization-specific content. The length of the sentence and the amount of time allowed for counting determine the difficulty of the task.

Usage   Group: Date:
                Comments:

                Group: Date:
                Comments:

                Group: Date:
                Comments:

                Group: Date:
                Comments:

                Group: Date:
                Comments:

Ideas for Variations

ELEPHANTS AND GIRAFFES

Summary Participant who is "it" attempts to get out of the center of the circle by getting someone to make a mistake.

Preparation None

Procedure

1. Assemble the group in a large circle, an arm's length apart. Take the part of "it" in the center of the circle.

2. Explain that the object of this game is to have fun. The method is to get someone to make a mistake in order for the person who is "it" to get out of the center.

3. Name the game "Elephants and Giraffes," and explain that when you point to an individual and say "elephant," that person has to use his/her hands to make the long snout of the elephant. (Demonstrate by making fists that you add to your nose.) The individuals on each side of that person must use their hands to attach an elephant's big ear to each side of the person being pointed at. (Demonstrate with a volunteer by making a kind of fan with your hands, extending the size of one of that person's ears.) All this has to happen before the person in the middle of the circle counts out loud to three. Pick someone and demonstrate by saying, "Elephant one, two, three!" (About one second per word.) Answer questions and be prepared to demonstrate the elephant again, perhaps with other people.

4. Next, demonstrate "giraffe" by explaining that the person pointed to must raise his/her arms to a point above the head to make the giraffe's long neck. The individuals on either side must stoop, facing forward, and hold onto the ankle of the person in the middle, making the lower body of the giraffe. Point at someone and say, "Giraffe one, two, three!" Answer any questions.

5. Start the game. Continue until someone makes a mistake. Change positions with that person who then selects someone else to point to. (Part of the fun is that people in the center often forget to count.)

Cautions   None

Variations   • Other animals can be used. The group can make up its own portrayals of animals.

• More than one person can be in the middle at one time. Of course, they may not involve the same three participants simultaneously.

Usage   Group: Date:
Comments:

Group: Date:
Comments:

Group: Date:
Comments:

Group: Date:
Comments:

Group: Date:
Comments:

Ideas for Variations

FANTASY OBJECT

Summary Participants stand in a circle and play with an imaginary object.

Preparation None

Procedure

1. Assemble the group in a circle and announce that the next activity will be playful, quick, and imaginary. Also, it will be totally non-verbal — that is, no talking. The only other rule is that you must have fun!

2. Explain that in a moment you are going to place a "fantasy substance" on the floor in the center of the circle. Someone is to pick it up, make something out of it rapidly, and present it to another group member in an expressive manner. That person then re-forms the object and makes a quick presentation to a third person. The activity will continue until all participants have made something out of the substance.

3. Walk to the center and pretend to place the substance on the floor. Rejoin the circle and participate. Ask for a volunteer to begin.

4. After all have participated, stop the activity and promote a brief discussion. Individuals may want to say what they were attempting to portray or express. Others may want to talk about receiving the object.

Cautions None

Variations

- The object can simply be passed to the person on the right. This speeds up the process, but it is less fun. Afterwards, talk about what was made out of the substance.

- The entire activity can be carried out *with* talking. People can guess what is being made by each person.

Usage   Group: Date:
             Comments:

             Group: Date:
             Comments:

             Group: Date:
             Comments:

             Group: Date:
             Comments:

             Group: Date:
             Comments:

Ideas for Variations

IMAGINARY BALL GAME

Summary   Participants invent a ball game and play it — all without using words.

Preparation   Obtain a soft ball such as a tennis, soccer, or "Nerf" ball.

Procedure

1. Assemble the group in a circle. Explain that before going into the next part of the program everyone will play a completely new game.

2. Toss the ball into the center of the circle. Announce that the group's task is to create and play a ball game. There are only two rules established beforehand: you may not use words, and you must have fun!

3. Let the process begin. (You may need to point to someone to coax him/her into picking up the ball.)

4. After a few minutes stop the game and ask the group to talk about it.

Cautions   None

Variations

- You can permit talking during the creation phase.

- You can set a limit on the number of minutes for inventing the game.

- You can stipulate that the game must (or must not) be competitive.

Usage   Group: Date:
Comments:

Group: Date:
Comments:

Group: Date:
Comments:

Group: Date:
Comments:

Group: Date:
Comments:

Ideas for Variations

I-ME-MINE

Summary   This is a dyadic communication contest in which participants attempt to avoid using first-person pronouns.

Preparation   Generate a list of controversial topics. These may be current events issues, organizational situations, or general topics such as abortion, the budget deficit, aid to the homeless, etc. You may want to make a poster or overhead transparency that shows the list.

Procedure   1. Remind the group of the English parts of speech (nouns, pronouns, verbs, adverbs, adjectives, prepositions, conjunctions, and interjections). Ask for a definition of a pronoun (a word that takes the place of a noun). Ask for a definition of first, second, and third person pronouns (first: I, we, etc.; second: you, your, etc.; third: he, it, they, etc.). Then make a list of all first-person pronouns, singular and plural, on a flipchart, whiteboard, or overhead transparency. Here is the list, which you may want to post:

I	we
me	us
my	our
mine	ours
myself	ourselves.

2. Explain that the game that they are about to play, "I-Me-Mine," is a communications exercise that requires each person to have an opponent. Call for a volunteer to come to the front of the room to show how the game works.

3. Spell out the rules of the game. (You may want to post them.)

> 1. Have a two-way conversation on the assigned topic.
> 2. The conversation must make sense.
> 3. There can be no more than four seconds between when one finishes saying something and the other person responds.
> 4. You must say at least four words when it is your turn to speak.
> 5. You may not ask questions.
> 6. The opponent who says one of the first-person pronouns loses.

4. Pick a topic and demonstrate the game with the audience functioning as referee. Thank the volunteer and call for applause.

5. Have everyone pair up and play the game. Give everyone the same topic, different from the one you used in the demonstration.

Cautions Keep this energizer moving along briskly. If people are good at the game, declare ties. Move around and enjoy the interactions yourself.

Variations
- Winners can be told to find other winners and continue to play the game. You may even stage this as a tournament, with semifinals and finals staged in front of the entire group. Table teams can select their best players to enter the tournament.

- You can have a rich discussion after the game. The interaction can lead to such generalizations as our preoccupation with self, the need to get out of that mindset when attempting to influence others, etc.

- The group can generate its own list of controversial topics. Ask something like this: "On what topics are there likely to be strongly held differences of opinion inside this group?" The emotional loading on the topic increases the likelihood that a person will make the mistake of using a first-person pronoun.

- The entire game can be carried out with either second-person (confrontive) or third-person ("If it weren't for them…") pronouns.

Usage   Group: Date:

                 Comments:

                 Group: Date:

                 Comments:

                 Group: Date:

                 Comments:

                 Group: Date:

                 Comments:

                 Group: Date:

                 Comments:

Ideas for Variations

Adapted by permission from "I Down" exercise included in the Adventures in Attitudes program of Performax, Minneapolis, Minnesota.

JIGSAW PUZZLES

Summary   The group pieces together a large puzzle that contains the training event or conference themes.

Preparation   Get a large sheet of paper or poster board. Print (in large block letters) the themes of your training event or conference on the paper. Then cut it into more pieces than you have members in the total group.

Assemble piles of randomly selected pieces, one pile for each participant. Leftovers are placed in a separate pile.

Procedure   1. Announce that the group will cooperate to piece together a jigsaw puzzle. Have everyone come to the front and pick up a pile of pieces.

2. Point out that there are additional pieces in a small pile in the center of the room (a large open space).

3. Give a signal for the task to begin.

4. When the puzzle is assembled, have the group read the themes aloud, and call for a round of applause.

Cautions   None

Variations   You can prepare several puzzles, so that people have to sort out to which puzzle their pieces belong. This variation can be simplified by having puzzles with different colors.

Usage   Group: Date:
Comments:

Group: Date:
Comments:

Group: Date:
Comments:

Group: Date:
Comments:

Group: Date:
Comments:

Ideas for Variations

LEADERS' BIRTH SIGNS

Summary   Participants group according to Chinese birth signs and make fun presentations of themselves as leaders.

Preparation   Post the following twelve sets of birth years around the room. Do not include the name of the sign, only the years. Here are the lists:

(Rat)	1900, 1912, 1924, 1936, 1948, 1960, 1972
(Buffalo)	1901, 1913, 1925, 1937, 1949, 1961, 1973
(Tiger)	1902, 1914, 1926, 1938, 1950, 1962, 1974
(Cat)	1903, 1915, 1927, 1939, 1951, 1963, 1975
(Dragon)	1904, 1916, 1928, 1940, 1952, 1964, 1976
(Snake)	1905, 1917, 1929, 1941, 1953, 1965, 1977
(Horse)	1906, 1918, 1930, 1942, 1954, 1966, 1978
(Goat)	1907, 1919, 1931, 1943, 1955, 1967, 1979
(Monkey)	1908, 1920, 1932, 1944, 1956, 1968, 1980
(Rooster)	1909, 1921, 1933, 1945, 1957, 1969, 1981
(Dog)	1910, 1922, 1934, 1946, 1958, 1970, 1982
(Pig)	1911, 1923, 1935, 1947, 1959, 1971, 1983.

Procedure   1. Announce that before entering the next phase of the program the participants will learn some interesting things about one another. Point out the birth-year signs and instruct people to go to the sign that contains their year of birth and to greet the others who show up there.

2. After a minute or so announce that these birth-year signs represent the signs of the Chinese horoscope. Ask people to guess what their sign is. Request that participants who know their sign not reveal it to the other group members. Then announce the signs one by one. (This should get several laughs.)

3. Instruct the groups to come up with two positive leadership characteristics and one potential liability that leaders born under their sign possess.

4. Get a report from each group. Applaud after each one.

Cautions   Some people are offended by astrology and others take it seriously. Make sure that you play this activity lightly and quickly.

Variations
- You may wish to hand out to each group an interpretation of its sign. A good reference for such material is Paula Delsol's *Chinese Horoscopes* (London: Pan Books Ltd., 1973). This book contains the exact dates in each birth year that correspond to the signs, along with copious interpretation suggestions.

- In introducing the activity you could ask someone to ask your sign. Respond by saying, "I'm a Leo (Virgo, etc.) and Leo's don't believe in astrology!" Always good for a laugh, particularly in California. Groups can tell each other how they are likely to act in the remainder of the session based on their consciousness of their sign.

Usage   Group: Date:
Comments:

Group: Date:
Comments:

Group: Date:
Comments:

Group: Date:
Comments:

Group: Date:
Comments:

Ideas for Variations

LIMERICKS

Summary   Teams make up limericks and share them with one another.

Preparation   Make up a list of final words that teams will use as the basis for creating limericks. Examples: meant, fine, law, wages, etc.

Procedure   1. Form teams by counting off by the number of teams you want to establish (not the number of people in them).

2. Announce that these teams will have the task of composing a limerick, but first you will give an example:

> The limerick is furtive and mean.
> You must keep it in close quarantine,
> Or it sneaks to the slums
> And promptly becomes
> Disorderly, drunk, and obscene!

3. Point out that there are three beats in lines one, two, and five, which all rhyme. Lines three and four have two beats and rhyme with each other.

4. Assign a word to each team. This word must appear at the end of either lines one, two, or five of the team's limerick. Give teams five minutes to create their limericks.

5. Call for a recitation from each team, and applaud after each one.

Cautions   Because almost all limericks are, in fact, obscene, you want to make sure that this activity remains tasteful. Do not let members recite their favorites!

This energizer can consume quite a bit of time. Therefore, keep it moving briskly.

Variations   • Each team can create only one line of a limerick and pass it to another group, which must complete it.

- A "judge" from each team can form a panel to determine the winning limerick.

- Teams may rank-order the limericks from all teams but their own, from best to worst. These rankings can be summed to determine a winner.

- The limericks can be about the themes of the training event or conference.

Usage

Group: Date:
Comments:

Group: Date:
Comments:

Group: Date:
Comments:

Group: Date:
Comments:

Group: Date:
Comments:

Ideas for Variations

LINEUP

Summary   Without talking, participants form a straight line in the order of their influence in the group so far.

Preparation   None

Procedure   1. Announce that before going on with the program, it is time for the group to assess itself quickly.

2. Ask everyone to put away anything they may have in their hands and stand quietly.

3. Announce that the group will now line itself up, according to the influence that members have shown so far in the program. The line will face a wall. The person with the most influence will be closest to the wall; the others will line up one behind the other.

4. The rules are as follows: no talking; put yourself where you think you belong (not where you would like to be); move others if you do not agree; be nonviolent; and no ties — everyone must have his/her own position.

5. After the group has completed the line, form it into a semi-circle and lead a brief discussion of the experience.

Cautions   This task can be difficult for some groups. You may need to "sell" it in certain situations.

The discussion can be "heavy" in some cases. Be prepared to draw people out and confront the integrity of the choices made during the lineup.

Variations   • Any of the rules can be changed.

• The lineup criterion can be almost any topic, such as helpfulness, participation, commitment to the group's plan, etc.

- You may have people at the two ends of the line talk with each other briefly. Pair them up, and have people in the middle play the role of third-party consultants.

Usage   Group: Date:
            Comments:

            Group: Date:
            Comments:

            Group: Date:
            Comments:

            Group: Date:
            Comments:

            Group: Date:
            Comments:

Ideas for Variations

THE MACHINE

Summary   The group forms itself into a moving-and-sounding machine.

Preparation   None

Procedure
1. Assemble the group in a circle.

2. Announce that at this point in the program the group has become a well-oiled machine, so it is time to celebrate its development in a special, fun way.

3. Call for a volunteer to go to the center of the circle and to become a moving part of a machine, making the movement and sound that goes along with it.

4. Ask others to join the machine one by one, making the movement and sounds of different parts. Each participant must be connected with at least one of the other parts of the machine. Continue until everyone is part of the machine.

5. Then, instruct one part of the machine to malfunction. Then another. Finally, announce that you are about to "pull the plug" on the machine and that all of the parts will fall in a heap on the floor.

Cautions   Caution the first person not to make the movement strenuous or loud, because he/she will continue being that part until the entire machine stops.

Someone could get hurt when the machine collapses. Make sure that this is a gentle process.

Variations
• You could specify a particular kind of machine that the group will build, such as a loom, a lawn mower, or an office copier.

• Members can use objects from the room to supplement their machine.

• The machine can move about the room.

Usage   Group: Date:
             Comments:

             Group: Date:
             Comments:

             Group: Date:
             Comments:

             Group: Date:
             Comments:

             Group: Date:
             Comments:

Ideas for Variations

MARSHMALLOW TOSS

Summary   The group throws marshmallows to one another while in a circle.

Preparation   Buy a large bag of big marshmallows.

Procedure
1. Assemble the group in a circle. Tell them that they will be tossing marshmallows to other people in the circle. There are two rules: toss each marshmallow to a different member, and remember who tossed marshmallows to you.

2. Give a marshmallow to about four or five people and begin the process. When a person receives a marshmallow, he or she is to toss it to someone else.

3. After a few seconds stop the process and announce that the sequence will now be reversed. People will now throw marshmallows to the people who originally tossed the marshmallows to them.

4. After a few minutes, give everyone two or three marshmallows and let them toss them freely.

Cautions   None

Variations
- You can use other objects, such as plastic practice golf balls.
- You may omit the reverse toss and let the process be spontaneous.

Usage   Group: Date:
Comments:

Group: Date:
Comments:

Group: Date:
Comments:

Group: Date:
Comments:

Group: Date:
Comments:

Ideas for Variations

NEW GROUPS

Summary   New learning teams are formed by a quick, simple method.

Preparation None

Procedure   1. Explain that it is often rewarding to get to know people in the session in addition to those within one's learning team. Announce that new teams are about to be formed.

2. Decide how many new teams you would like to have. Go to each existing team and "number off" its members, from 1 through the number of new teams you want to form. Keep the sequence going from team to team. That is, if the final member of the first team happens to be 4, begin counting in the next team with the number 5.

3. Tell the group that in a moment you will form *temporary* new teams, which will be adjusted as needed. Explain that when you give the signal, everyone who has the number 1 will go to the back left corner of the room, 2's will go to the left front corner, etc. Ask them not to talk to or touch one another.

4. When the temporary groups are assembled, ask, "What adjustments do we need to make to balance these teams?" Of course, they may now talk in order to respond to your question. Have groups trade personnel to balance themselves.

5. Give the teams one minute to come up with a memorable name for themselves. Have each group present its new name energetically. Applaud after each presentation.

Cautions   The criteria for balancing the teams can become controversial. Keep this light and quick.

If the Trainer makes up the new teams, people can become suspicious. It is usually better to form teams randomly or to enlist the help of participants.

Variations
- A representative from each "old" team can join a committee to re-form the teams.

- Teams can make up logos, mottoes, and cheers.

Usage

Group: Date:
Comments:

Group: Date:
Comments:

Group: Date:
Comments:

Group: Date:
Comments:

Group: Date:
Comments:

Ideas for Variations

NOOGIE GAME

Summary   In an on-going game, teams compete for partial points called "noogies."

Preparation   Make up a score-keeping poster, with vertical columns headed by team names. A side column can be added for round numbers if desired.

Obtain a source of trivia, such as a box of Trivial Pursuit cards or information that none of the participants know about your organization.

Procedure   1. Announce that teams will compete for prizes that will be awarded on the basis of total points accumulated through several rounds of the Noogie Game. The game will be played periodically throughout the entire session. (The number of games and the scheduling is at the discretion of the Trainer). Reveal the score-keeping poster and explain that it is everyone's responsibility to make sure that the scores are correct at all times.

2. Define a noogie as half of a quarter of a point (mysteriously, not an eighth of a point, though). Two noogies make a quarter of a point. Scoring will be cumulative, and the prizes for final scores at the closing session will be significant.

3. Tell the participants that you are going to ask a trivia question. (You may ask one or more questions per round. In the first round, ask enough questions so that every team "gets on the board.") They will have 10 seconds, as a team, to decide on the answer. You will call time and have a spokesperson for each team stand and give its answer.

4 When all teams have responded, tell them the correct answer. Ask all teams who were correct to cheer and call out their team name. Award a "noogie" (recorded on the poster as a check mark) to each cheering team.

5. Ask one or more additional questions as desired and follow the above procedure. Then, convert the noogies to points. Remember, each team is responsible for accurate translation of noogies into points. Keep a running total for each team. After each round, cross through the previous total on the poster in order to write the new point total for each team as it scores.

> ### SCORING
> ✔ = 1/2 of 1/4 point (alone, it is not convertable to points — it does not equal 1/8 point)
> ✔ ✔ = 1/4 point
> ✔ ✔ ✔ = 1/4 point plus a noogie (✔) to accumulate towards points

6. Follow the same procedure for Round 2, continuing to keep a running point total for each team.

Cautions This energizer has the potential for consuming a lot of time, so keep it fast-paced with a lot of humor and cheering.

Avoid arguing about what answers are correct. Be the final judge.

Accept only fair "challenge" questions. For example, if a team is calling for an exact answer, instruct them to specify a range instead.

The negie noogie variation can put you into a cop role. Any time you feel uncomfortable, call for a vote, with majority rule.

Variations • The final session can feature "challenge trivia," questions submitted by each team to you. Each team challenges the remaining teams. The challenging team gets one noogie for each incorrect answer to its question. Correct answers, of course, result in noogies for those teams providing them. You may increase the number of noogies at risk for a given question in order to make it possible for a team to come from behind and win. For example, if the team scores are highly uneven before the challenge round, you may wish to make it at least theoretically possible for the last team to earn enough points to win the contest.

- Noogies can be used for crowd control. A team that has all of its members seated in place after a refreshment break can earn a punctuality noogie. Each team that has at least half of its members engage in at least thirty minutes of exercise in a day can earn a recreation noogie.

- Negie noogies, or subtractions, can result from any participant engaging in negative behavior, such as tardiness, sarcasm, buttering up the presenter, etc. A team that returns from a break too early could be penalized.

- Teams can earn noogies from other competitive activities, such as a ring toss, pitching coins into a cup, "Puttoff," etc.

Usage

Group: Date:
Comments:

Group: Date:
Comments:

Group: Date:
Comments:

Group: Date:
Comments:

Group: Date:
Comments:

Ideas for Variations

Adapted with permission from an exercise developed by Jack Carew, Carew Positional Selling Systems, Cincinnati, Ohio.

OWA TAGU SIAM

Summary   This is a group "chant," with a punch line.

Preparation   None

Procedure

1. Explain that before resuming the regular program the group will energize itself by doing a group chant. Have everyone sit straight in their chairs and prepare themselves mentally to engage in this ritual.

2. Point out that this chant has a secret meaning. It is from an Eastern rite (do not explain) that helps people purify and ready themselves for significant new experiences.

3. Explain that the chant will begin slowly and quietly, gradually building up speed and volume over about a minute. Everyone will do the chant together, with the same pacing and loudness.

4. Recite the chant slowly, one word at a time, clearly spaced apart so that people do not get its meaning. (OWA TAGU SIAM = Oh, what a goose I am!) Have the group practice chanting each word separately to imprint them as "words" in their minds.

5. Start the group chant. As the pace and volume increases, some participants will figure out the punchline. Stop the chant and have a good laugh with them.

Cautions   Do not play this as a religious rite. Some participants may be offended.

Variations

- Make up different chants with other phrases.

- Have a volunteer do the chant.

- A variation with completely different content is the "traffic signal." Have the group spell the word "stop" several times, in spelling-bee fashion (S-T-O-P). Then quickly ask, "What do you do at a green light?" Some will say, "Stop." Tell them you have fooled their "thinkers."

Usage Group: Date:
         Comments:

         Group: Date:
         Comments:

         Group: Date:
         Comments:

         Group: Date:
         Comments:

         Group: Date:
         Comments:

Ideas for Variations

PEOPLE TO PEOPLE

Summary   Participants select a series of partners and do nonverbal activities with them, usually involving physical touch. This is a high-energy, fun activity that involves physical movement and group mixing. It is best used after participants are reasonably comfortable with one another.

Preparation   None

Procedure

1. If there is an odd number of participants, ask one to stand aside while the process is demonstrated. Then that person can conduct the next round.

2. Explain that the entire activity will be *nonverbal,* that is, there will be no talking throughout. (It is sometimes useful, with a loquacious group, to invite participants to get all of their talking needs met before the game begins.) Further explain that when the phrase "People to people" is heard, everyone is to pair up with a new person — one they have not previously paired with during the game.

3. Start the game by saying, "People to people!" Everyone stands face-to-face with a partner. Then say, "Knees to knees" or "Elbows to elbows," etc. Partners must hold that pose until the "People to people" phrase is heard again. Then they scramble to find a new partner.

4. The odd person out then gives one or two commands (pausing after each to let people do the activity) before saying, "People to people." The commands may be cumulative, such as, "Back to back. [Pause.] Arms locked."

5. Participants will find it increasingly difficult to locate a new partner. Stop the process when almost all possible partnerships have been experienced.

Cautions   Some people are put off by being touched. Invite them to observe. Our experience with this energizer is that it rises to the readiness level of its user. If you feel tense in introducing it, it will not be as much fun as it might be under the direction of someone else.

Variations   Instead of physical touch, the entire activity can require various "acting-out" behaviors, such as making faces at each other, expressing various emotions, or communicating about their relationship without using words.

Usage   Group: Date:
Comments:

Group: Date:
Comments:

Group: Date:
Comments:

Group: Date:
Comments:

Group: Date:
Comments:

Ideas for Variations

PERSONAL STYLE PROJECTIVE TEST

Summary   This energizer is a kind of joke, with a "sting" at the end. It is a paper-and-pencil activity in which participants assess themselves.

Preparation   Make sure that everyone has paper and pencils or pens.

Procedure

1. Announce that before you move on to the next part of the program, you will pause to take inventory of the group. Ask everyone to get writing material ready for a very interesting quiz.

2. When everyone is ready, point out that there is a type of personality test called "projective." The most famous example is the Rorschach Ink-Blot Test. Ask for a show of hands of those who are familiar with this test. Explain that you will be administering a similar test, but not on personality. This one will focus on *style in approaching problems*.

3. Instruct everyone neither to talk nor look at anyone else's paper during the test. Then tell them to draw four symbols on their paper, about the same size each. The four symbols are a circle, a square, a triangle, and the letter Z.

4. Explain that now they are to rank-order these four symbols according to how they represent their own approach to solving problems. They are to write a "1" beside the symbol most like their approach, a "2" by the second most like them, and so on. Allow no questions.

5. Now you will interpret the results. (Keep this part serious, because you are setting up the punch line.) Ask for a show of hands of the people who ranked the circle first, that is, most like their approach to solving problems. Invite others to see whose hands are raised. Point out that this symbol indicates an emphasis on Holistic Thinking. (Say whatever you like in defining the term, such as keeping things in perspective, getting the whole picture, etc.) Have the people raise their hands again, and repeat the interpretive name of the symbol.

6. Call for a show of the hands of people who ranked the square first, and invite others to observe who chose that symbol. Tell them that this symbol represents Emergent Leadership. Explain this idea in your own terms, such as the Managerial Grid, Situational Leadership, or whatever. Ask them to raise their hands again, and repeat the symbol's interpretive name.

7. Get a show of hands of the people who ranked the triangle number one. Name this symbol Analytical Detachment, and elaborate on it briefly (considering all the angles, Machiavellian in approach, stable configuration, etc.). Ask for a show of hands again and repeat the interpretive name.

8. Finally, ask for the hands of people who ranked the Z number 1. Then ask them to stand so that everyone can see them clearly. When they are all standing, point out that this symbol denotes a preoccupation with sex and booze (or other "sting" of your choice.)

9. Lead a round of applause.

Cautions   Some people take this activity seriously because you stage it as a real self-assessment. Make sure that they understand afterwards that there is absolutely no validity to the so-called test.

Occasionally someone is offended by the punch line, especially if they are standing at the end. If you are aware of such a person in the group, ask them privately not to participate.

Variations   • You can name these symbols according to your pet models of leadership, communication, or relationships. Also, the test can be about almost any topic other than your approach to solving problems.

• You can use other symbols, such as a diamond, trapezoid, heart, etc.

Usage   Group: Date:
            Comments:

            Group: Date:
            Comments:

            Group: Date:
            Comments:

            Group: Date:
            Comments:

            Group: Date:
            Comments:

Ideas for Variations

PICKET SIGNS

Summary   Individuals create personal picket signs and march with them.

Preparation   Assemble felt-tipped pens, large pieces of cardboard, picket sticks, and fastening devices.

Procedure   1. Announce that before getting into the next phase of the program everyone will canvass the group in a special way. Explain that individuals will construct picket signs that give their strongly-held personal points of view about the upcoming topic. These could be slogans, pithy statements, or drawings that can be quickly and perfectly understood by anyone who sees them.

2. Distribute the construction materials and allow five to ten minutes for people to make their signs. When almost everyone has finished making their signs, announce that they will now mill about the room (not parade formally) and picket each other on the topic (about five minutes). Boisterous reactions are acceptable.

3. Lead a brief discussion of the experience, making a transition into the next part of your program.

Cautions   This can be a contentious energizer. Use it with care.

Avoid having people stereotype each other.

Do not, of course, use this activity if the participants' organization(s) is in (or anticipates or has recently settled) a labor-relations or contract-negotiations disagreement.

Variations   • The content of the signs can be made all positive by instructing participants to make signs that tell what they like best about working in their organization(s).

• Each team can make one picket sign.

- People who feel neutral can opt not to make signs. They can vote afterwards on whether they favor one side or the other.

- Picket signs can be pre-made, and people can choose those which appeal to them.

- People on opposite sides may caucus before picketing. They can form lines, even cross each other's lines.

Usage   Group: Date:
Comments:

Group: Date:
Comments:

Group: Date:
Comments:

Group: Date:
Comments:

Group: Date:
Comments:

Ideas for Variations

PUNCH LINES

Summary   Pairs of participants find each other and tell jokes to the group.

Preparation   Obtain a set of tasteful jokes, and select a number greater than your number of participants. Print a set of two cards for each joke — the setup and the punch line. Shuffle the cards.

Procedure   1.   Tell the group that before moving into the next part of the program they will have a "laugh" session. Explain that you will be distributing cards, half of which state only the beginnings of jokes, the other half only the punch lines. Their task will be to find the person who has the other half of their joke — without talking — and prepare to tell it to the entire group. Ask the participants not to read their cards aloud until they have found their partners and gone off to a private place to rehearse their joke.

2.   Give a signal to begin. When everyone is paired up and has rehearsed their joke telling, call for a recitation of the jokes, preferably in the participants' own words. (Jokes read aloud are often not funny.) Finally, get a round of applause for the group's accomplishment of the task.

Cautions   Keep this energizer tasteful. Do not select jokes that put anyone down. No "isms" such as sexism, ageism, racism, etc. (As one wag said, "I'm waiting for the day when all isms become wasms.")

Variations   •   Members can submit their favorite tasteful jokes to you for use in the energizer.

•   Before calling for the recitations you may wish to tell the story about joke telling in the insane asylum. A visitor heard the patients calling out numbers in the cafeteria. Each time the patients would laugh uproariously. The visitor asked the host, "What are they laughing at?" The host replied, "They're telling jokes from the institution's joke book. Everyone knows them, so they only tell the numbers." The visitor stood up and called out a number. No one laughed. His host pointed out that some people just can't tell jokes.

• Instead of jokes you can use famous sayings and their authors.

Usage   Group: Date:
Comments:

Group: Date:
Comments:

Group: Date:
Comments:

Group: Date:
Comments:

Group: Date:
Comments:

Ideas for Variations

PUTTOFF

Summary   This activity involves teams of participants competing in a golf putting contest. Several rounds of the contest can be held during a training event with prizes for the winning team based on a cumulative score.

Preparation   Set up a putting area, on carpet, with the charts (directions to follow) posted near by. The scoring areas are lined off on the carpet with masking tape. A styrofoam coffee cup (with the bottom cut out) is secured at the center with masking tape. (See the diagram below.)

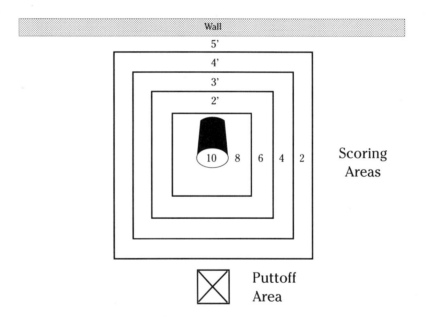

Count off about twenty feet from the front of the cup and place a line of tape to designate from where the participants must putt. Obtain a golf putter (preferably one that can be used by either right- or left-handed participants) and two golf balls.

Prepare a blank chart for *each* team that will show the putting order of the members and will be used to collect the individual points for each round. The information will be filled in by the teams.

CHIEFS							
Rounds							
Putting Order	**1**	**2**	**3**	**4**	**5**	**6**	**7**
John							
Sue							
Bob							
Jill							
Mary							
Tom							
Total							

Using team names, make a master scoring chart to record the teams' total scores for each round. The Trainer should fill in this information.

PUTTOFF SCORES					
T E A M S					
Round	Chiefs	Aces	Tops	Go-gos	Bosses
1					
2					
3					
4					
5					
6					
7					
TOTAL					

Make a poster of the "Puttoff" rules, listed below.

PUTTOFF RULES
- Every member of each team must putt each round.
- The second ball scores; the first is practice.
- Play rotates across teams, member by member.
- You may not physically interfere with anyone's putt.
- You must have fun.

Make a chart of the scoring points.

POINTS

20 = Through the cup, hitting the wall, back through cup from rear

10 = Through the cup

8 = Resting in center area (#8)

6 = Resting in center area (#6)

4 = Resting in center area (#4)

2 = Resting in center area (#2)

On the line = the higher score

Post all the charts on the walls near the puttoff area.

Procedure

1. Assemble the entire group in the puttoff area and explain the game, calling attention to the rules. Point out that these are the only rules. (It is permissible to cheer and boo.)

2. Instruct teams to determine quickly the order of their putting. Have a person from each team write on their team chart the member's names in the order in which they will putt.

3. Conduct Round 1, calling up Member 1 from Team 1, Member 1 from Team 2, etc., until all have putted. Have the teams record the score as each participant putts.

4. Total the points for each team for Round 1 and enter the total on the bottom of each team chart and at Round 1 of the Puttoff Scores chart.

5. Additional rounds should be conducted throughout the program at the Trainer's discretion.

6. The team with the highest cumulative total at the end of the session wins. Pass out an appropriate prize and call for a round of applause.

Cautions

This activity can take a lot of time, so it must be run efficiently. Avoid the temptation to stretch it out. Keep everyone actively involved. Some can keep score, some can call up the next person to putt, others can be cheerleaders, etc.

Variations
- Use only one ball. This speeds up the activity. We often take away the practice ball after Round 1. Encourage people to practice during refreshment breaks.

- Teams may select their best golfer to represent the team, rather than have everyone putt. Remaining team members can cheer on their representatives.

- In the final round you can place a barrier in the putting path. You may even hide the cup with a cloth curtain.

Usage

Group: Date:
Comments:

Group: Date:
Comments:

Group: Date:
Comments:

Group: Date:
Comments:

Group: Date:
Comments:

Ideas for Variations

QUICK ASSOCIATION QUIZ

Summary   Participants discover their habitual ways of thinking through the use of a brief paper-and-pencil exercise.

Preparation   Make sure that everyone has paper and a pencil or pen.

Procedure   1. Announce that the next activity will be a pop quiz. Tell everyone to get out a piece of paper and write down the numbers from one through five. Explain that this is not a spelling test. Tell them that this will be a six-item quiz but that the final item will be non-verbal.

2. Administer the quiz orally (and quickly):

   1. Write down the first color that comes into your mind.
   2. Write the name of the first automobile you think of.
   3. Write down the name of the first flower that occurs to you.
   4. Write the name of the first foreign country you think of.
   5. Write the name of the first piece of furniture that comes to mind.

3. Explain that before going on to the sixth and final item, everyone will score the first five items.

4. Ask for a show of hands of people who wrote "red" for Item 1 (this will almost always be a majority). Then ask for hands of people who wrote "blue." Then ask them to keep their hands raised while those who responded "red" raise theirs also (usually this is almost everyone).

5. Now score Item 3. Get a show of hands for participants who wrote "rose."

6. Ask for a show of hands for those who wrote "chair" for Item 5. Explain that Items 2 and 4 are not scored. They are fillers, or distracters, to disguise the real nature of the test.

7. Point out that red, rose, and chair are the normal responses.

8. Now explain the final, nonverbal item. Ask everyone to fold their arms (if they are not already doing so). Ask how this feels. (Most will say something like "comfortable.") Now tell them to fold their arms the other way. Do it yourself, and fumble a bit in the process. Ask how this feels. (Most will say things like "awkward," "uncomfortable," "not sure I'm doing it right," etc.) Have everyone now fold their arms the familiar way and ask how it feels. ("Better," "right," "comfortable," etc.)

9. Point out that this is how change feels — uncomfortable. When we are forced out of our "red-rose-chair" orientations, we are put off, de-skilled. Leaders need to be sensitive to this effect of change on their followers.

Cautions   Do not get preachy about the implications of the change phenomenon.

Variations
- Omit Items 2 and 4 to speed up the activity.

- You may eliminate the nonverbal item.

- You may interpret the verbal items as telling us that we are all caught up in habitual ways of thinking. We need to "get out of the nine dots" to change.

- Ask participants to do the interpretation. Ask something like this: "What does this test tell us?"

Usage   Group: Date:
Comments:

Group: Date:
Comments:

Group: Date:
Comments:

Group: Date:
Comments:

Group: Date:
Comments:

Ideas for Variations

REINCARNATED ANIMALS

Summary   Teams act out extinct animals, and others attempt to guess what animals are being portrayed.

Preparation   None

Procedure
1. Announce that the next activity will be a team competition. Explain that each group will choose an extinct animal and portray it nonverbally. The other teams will then attempt to guess what animal is being portrayed.

2. Give teams five minutes to prepare their presentations.

3. Ask each team to act out its animal. Call for guesses. The acting team announces the winner as soon as someone guesses it correctly (applause). If no one guesses the correct name, the acting team gives the answer (applause).

Cautions   None

Variations
- The animals can be non-extinct.

- Famous people can be substituted for animals.

Usage   Group: Date:
Comments:

Group: Date:
Comments:

Group: Date:
Comments:

Group: Date:
Comments:

Group: Date:
Comments:

Ideas for Variations

SCREAM

Summary   The group stands and screams as loudly as possible for a few seconds.

Preparation   None

Procedure
1. Ask the participants to stand, and explain that before moving on everyone needs to become energized.

2. Instruct them to begin screaming "at the top of their lungs." Urge them to do it even louder. Then halt the process.

Cautions   Do not let this activity go on for more than a few seconds. Someone could harm their larynx.

Make sure you will not be disturbing others in the building. (We used this energizer once because a company that was in competition with our client was having a noisy meeting in the next ballroom. They retaliated with an even louder scream!)

Variations
- You may have a phrase to scream or a topic to scream about.

- Groups may attempt to out-scream each other.

Usage   Group: Date:
Comments:

Group: Date:
Comments:

Group: Date:
Comments:

Group: Date:
Comments:

Group: Date:
Comments:

Ideas for Variations

SIMON SAYS

Summary   The group follows instructions for brief physical exercise.

Preparation   None

Procedure   1. Have the group stand, and announce that now you are Simon the Commander.

   2. Conduct a rapid series of physical exercises such as, "Simon says (pause) jump up and down on your right foot," "...touch your toes," "...massage someone's shoulders," etc.

Cautions   Encourage people to find their own level of participation in this energizer. Tell them to do what they can and avoid what they are not supposed to do for physical safety reasons.

Variations   • Have the group line up, all facing the same way. Then have them massage the shoulders (neck) of the person in front of them. After a minute or so, have them turn around and return the favor.

   • Get the group into a circle, and pass the role of Simon to the left after each exercise.

Usage   Group: Date:
   Comments:

   Group: Date:
   Comments:

   Group: Date:
   Comments:

Group: Date:
Comments:

Group: Date:
Comments:

Ideas for Variations

SNAKE LINE

Summary   Participants form a line, hold hands, and "snake" though the room.

Preparation None

Procedure   1. Have everyone form a long line, shoulder to shoulder. (Become the first in line yourself.) Announce that this will be a "snake line" that will wind its way through the room. Tell everyone to take the hand of the person on their left and hold on throughout the movement.

2. Lead the group over, under, around, and through things. Laugh as you go. Wind the group into a coil at the end.

Cautions   Keep this energizer moving quickly, but be mindful of safety.

Have one or more volunteers serve as safety officers to prevent accidents.

Variations   • Form a conga line with everyone facing one way, hands on the waist of the person in front of them.

• Have the group sing as it goes.

• Play conga music during the activity.

Usage   Group: Date:
Comments:

Group: Date:
Comments:

Group: Date:
Comments:

Group: Date:
Comments:

Group: Date:
Comments:

Ideas for Variations

Dr. John E. Jones and Dr. William L. Bearley

SOFT OBJECTS

Summary   Participants throw soft objects to one another while energetic music plays.

Preparation   Obtain several soft objects, such as Nerf balls, Nerf Frisbees, beach balls, etc., that can be thrown without harm.

Arrange for energetic music to be played during the activity.

Procedure   1. Turn on the music, throw the objects to different individuals, and enjoy what happens. Clap to the music.

2. When the music stops, get a round of applause.

Cautions   Be prepared to be seen as a party pooper when you "pull the plug" on this energizer.

Do not overuse this activity. It gets old quickly.

Variations   • Form two groups and let them throw the objects to each other across an empty space.

• Encourage dancing in place while the music plays.

Usage   Group: Date:
Comments:

Group: Date:
Comments:

Group: Date:
Comments:

Group: Date:
Comments:

Group: Date:
Comments:

Ideas for Variations

SUPERLATIVES

Summary   Individuals present themselves in terms of superlative adjectives.

Preparation   None

Procedure

1. Have the group brainstorm adjectives that could describe the people present. Have one or two volunteers post the list while you keep the process going.

2. Instruct participants to select one attribute (or think of another) that they think they have more of than anyone else present. You may remind them of the three forms of adjectives: normal, comparative, and superlative (for example, good/better/best). Point out that some superlatives are formed by adding the word "most" in front. If they cannot think of a superlative, they should choose a comparative. Then, form a sentence such as, "I am the happiest person here." Or, "I am happier than most people here."

3. Call for individuals to stand and give their sentences enthusiastically. Get applause after each presentation.

Cautions   None

Variations

- Make the superlatives relate to the entire organization rather than just the group.

- Change the activity to use the phrase, "I am the person who has the most..."

Usage   Group: Date:
Comments:

Group: Date:
Comments:

Group: Date:
Comments:

Group: Date:
Comments:

Group: Date:
Comments:

Ideas for Variations

TIMED TEST

Summary   Participants who do not follow directions precisely make mistakes in a paper-and-pencil activity that involves slight physical movement.

Preparation   Duplicate the test items (revise them as you wish). Make a copy for each participant. Provide pencils or pens.

Procedure   1. Introduce the activity by saying something like this: "Before we go on to the next part of our program, we need to take a test. Everyone get a pencil or pen ready."

2. With a straight face distribute the papers and instruct participants to read and follow the instructions.

Timed Test

Instructions: This is a test. The questions are numbered from 1-10. You are being timed on this test, so speed is important. Do exactly what each question asks you to do. Now, start and do questions one and ten. When you are finished, turn your paper over.

1. Write your name — first, middle, and last.
2. Add 89763 and 72868.
3. Subtract 94382 from 994382.
4. Stand up and sit down.
5. Clap your hands two times.
6. Say "Hi!" to your neighbor.
7. Write the last five letters of the alphabet.
8. Say these words: "I'm almost finished! I've followed directions."
9. Multiply 839 by 768.
10. Write your address backwards.

SMILE! TURN YOUR PAPER OVER!

Cautions   You must introduce this energizer in a convincing way. Remain sober until almost everyone has "completed" the assignment. Then laugh with them, and get them to talk about how some did not follow the directions. (Remember: they were only supposed to do items 1 and 10.)

Variations   You can edit the content of the test to include whatever you wish. You may want to make some of the items organization-specific, such as instructing people to chant the company motto three times in a loud, convincing voice.

Usage   Group: Date:
Comments:

Group: Date:
Comments:

Group: Date:
Comments:

Group: Date:
Comments:

Group: Date:
Comments:

Ideas for Variations

TROLLEY

Summary   Teams "ride" on "trolleys" in competition with one another.

Preparation   For each team make two "walking boards" out of 4x4's, ten feet long. Each board has five 4-foot ropes coming through the boards from the bottom to the top, with a loop at the top of the rope big enough to put a hand through. Countersink the underneath and top of the holes, and knot the ropes securely after inserting them into these holes. You may want to glue the knots into place and wrap the loops at the top with tape.

Lay out two parallel boards per team at one end of the staging area. (This activity can take place in a parking lot or indoors in a large room.)

Procedure   1. Assemble teams in the staging area and explain that this will be a competitive activity. The first "ride" will be for practice. Ask each team to select five members to "ride the trolley." Have these members put one foot on each of the boards and hold onto a rope coming up from each board. Have the teams then pull on the ropes while "walking" to the other end of the designated area. They may substitute other members at any time.

2. When they get to the end of area, stop the walking process and answer any questions.

3. Instruct the teams to remount their trollies and go in the opposite direction, back to their original spot. When all are back, announce that the competition is about to begin. Teams will traverse the same territory, turn around, and return, in a race with the other teams.

4. Give the signal to begin.

5. Get a round of applause for the winning team.

Cautions   People could fall off the boards, so remaining members can function as spotters.

This energizer can be time-consuming; pace it quickly.

Variations
- You can speed up this activity by eliminating the practice round, by making the race only the return leg of the course, or by not requiring that teams turn around while on the trolley.

- During the second round only one team member (on or off the trolley) may speak.

- You may require that every member of the team ride on the trolley at least part of the way.

- You may change the length of the boards, cutting down on the number of riders at any one time.

- Special recognition may be awarded to the winning team and the one that improved the most.

Usage
Group: Date:
Comments:

Group: Date:
Comments:

Group: Date:
Comments:

Group: Date:
Comments:

Group: Date:
Comments:

Ideas for Variations

VELVET BRICK REVIEW

Summary   Participants engage in a course review while paying close attention to receiving an object that is being thrown to them.

Preparation   Wrap an ordinary brick in velvet cloth, using strong glue. Prepare a list of review questions on the information that you have covered in your course up to this point.

Procedure
1. Announce that before moving on to new material and activities, you want to conduct a high-energy review of what has been covered so far.

2. Show the velvet brick. Explain that you are going to ask a review question and then toss the velvet brick to someone. They are to answer. If the answer is incorrect (you and the group decide), they are to toss the brick gently to someone else. (Repeat the question before the toss.) That person then replies. If the person answers correctly, give another review question before the toss. Continue through your review list.

Cautions   Someone could get hurt by the tossed object. Encourage people to be gentle.

Variations
- Teams can develop the list of review questions and toss the brick to other teams.

- You can use something besides a brick, such as a soft object.

- You can use the process for something besides course review, such as giving opinions on a topic.

Usage   Group: Date:
Comments:

Group: Date:
Comments:

Group: Date:
Comments:

Group: Date:
Comments:

Group: Date:
Comments:

Ideas for Variations

Further Reading

Hart, L. B. (1989). *Saying hello: Getting your group started.* King of Prussia, PA: Organization Design and Development.

Pfeiffer, J. W., and Jones, J. E. (1974-1981) *A handbook of structured experiences for human relations training.* Volumes I-VIII. San Diego, CA: University Associates.

Pfeiffer, J. W., and Jones, J. E. (1972-1981). *The annual handbook for group facilitators.* San Diego, CA: University Associates.

Notes

Notes

Notes